First Edition

Copyright © 2016 by Daniel Hogan

This book is dedicated to Bart, who not only taught me what works at work but also what it means to be a true friend.

Special thanks to my sister Sarah and to my parents, Ned and Connie, for inspiring me to write something longer than an email.

TABLE OF CONTENTS

INTRODUCTION

When I started my first job after graduating from college, I received precisely five minutes of instruction. The first four were focused on how to book a conference room. The last was consumed by an offhanded comment, which turned out to be one of the better pieces of career advice I've received in the last twenty years. "Oh, and don't piss off the admins," my outgoing counterpart explained. "I got on Deanna's bad side a long time ago and, well, I would not recommend it."

By nature I am an observer. For a long time I have watched new employees succeed, and I have watched them fail. I have seen the most brilliant minds fall flat on their faces, and I have also witnessed the severely disadvantaged become incredibly successful. I do not believe there is a single answer to what leads to career success, and as a result, the canon of business literature is vast. There are so many great ideas, in fact, that for someone just starting out in the business world, it can be a bit challenging to figure out where to start.

There are also diminishing returns when it comes to many of the topics covered in popular business books. For example, it may be helpful to read about a method for optimizing your time, but reading 200 pages worth of time-saving advice seems like an oxymoron.

The objective of this book is to provide some practical insight into the habits and practices that will help you get up to speed quickly and be successful in an early-career role. Many of the principles are universal, even outside the workplace, but this book is written principally for those in their first few years working in a professional capacity.

Every chapter contains insights I wish I had when I first started my career, and many of them are things that I am still working on and find that I need to be reminded of on a regular basis.

Although names or other identifying details have been changed in many instances, each anecdote is true and based on my first-hand experience. The purpose of this book is not to develop or convey theories about how the world works. It is simply to give you an early glimpse into the things I believe that sooner or later you will end up learning by your own experience.

When you're first starting out, it's natural to feel like a tiny mouse, at risk of being trampled at any moment by the giant corporate elephants roaming the halls. Contrary to popular fiction, elephants are not scared of mice. At best they seem to be annoyed by them.

One day however, you may wake up and realize that you've become one of the elephants. I hope that this book will prove useful during that transformation, and that one day you'll be inspired to share what you've learned as well.

Say Thank You

Piglet noticed that even though he had a Very Small Heart, it could hold a rather large amount of Gratitude.

– A. A. Milne, Winnie-the-Pooh

Some habits can cover a multitude of shortcomings. Saying thank you is one of them. When you say thank you, people will be more accessible, more helpful and more forgiving.

It's hard to think of a time when it's inappropriate to say thank you, so say it whenever you get the chance. It doesn't matter if people are just doing their jobs. For example, there might be someone at work who orders lunch for the team. It doesn't matter if that's listed on page one of his job description – thank him as if he's delivered a cold drink to you in the middle of the desert.

Thank people for showing up to meetings and joining phone calls. Thank your suppliers for doing what you've paid them to do. Thank your family for supporting you in your job. Thank people for telling you when you do something stupid, and thank them when they give you praise.

Thank your boss when she gives you feedback, even if it's not what you want to hear. If you're not sure how to phrase it, say "Thank you for letting me know how you feel. I'll work on it."

Every once in a while, write a personal thank-you note. Buy a set of quality notecards, grab a decent pen, and write a short note, making sure to express your gratitude for something specific that they've done.

I once had someone working for me who had recently graduated from college, and was assigned to our group even though she didn't have much experience. I'd been through this before and it didn't end well. She was different. As I look back on it the difference was a willing attitude and a wonderful, warm way of saying thank you.

On more than one occasion I called her into my office and asked her to complete what could only have seemed like an impossible task. Each time her eyes would get a bit wider, she would smile excitedly, and then she'd say something like "Thank you so much for letting me do this! I can't wait to start figuring this out!" I gave her more chances to figure things out, because I believed that she was sincere, and that she was grateful for the opportunity to learn.

The more you say thank you, the more people realize that you care about what they do. When they understand that you care about what they're doing, they'll be more likely to help you with your work and do a great job on the things that you need them to do.

Saying thank you also develops your ability to see what's good in each situation. Alphonse Karr wrote, "Some people grumble that roses have thorns; I am grateful that thorns have roses." It doesn't take any particular talent to sit around complaining about the thorns. Go find whoever planted the roses and say thank you.

Manage Your Tasks

Do the difficult things while they are easy and do the great things while they are small.

– Lao Tzu

Sometimes it's nice to have other people do things for you; however, managing what you do with your time should not be one of them. Others will gravitate toward what's best for them, while you must diligently fight for the things that are important to you and to your long-term objectives.

Regardless of who may make demands on your time, including your manager, you are ultimately responsible for tracking your own priorities, requests, commitments and schedule. If you abandon this charge, you are leaving the castle walls undefended, and eventually the barbarian hordes will come and take over your calendar.

At times it may seem as though you have no choice over what you do and when. You may be called into mandatory meetings, or have assignments dumped on you without any regard for what else you have on your plate. Sometimes you literally just can't control the requests that come your way.

Many – consciously or otherwise – use this as a rationale for not managing their commitments at all. "My schedule is so nuts, it's not even worth trying," they'll say. But in fact, the more chaotic your schedule and set of assignments are, the more you need a way to manage everything.

When things are calm, or if your responsibilities are fairly straightforward, you might be able to get away with just a piece of paper on which to write down what you need to do, and cross it off when it's complete. However, most people can benefit from something a bit more sophisticated. Reading any number of the excellent books on the subject may be helpful. My favorite is Paul Allen's *Getting Things Done*. You may prefer a different approach. There are also a number of technological solutions based on his method and others, which you might find more convenient than old-fashioned paper-based methods.

What's important is to find a method that works for you, and then stick to it especially when things get rough. When you get overloaded, you'll need to have something that clearly and accurately shows what you've been asked to do, and where you're currently focusing. Using this, work with your manager and others to prioritize your workload and get things under control. Even your most abusive requestors will help you prioritize if you can show them that it will make you more productive, and hence more valuable to them in the long run.

It takes real commitment to keep up this process day in and day out, and it takes time away from your already busy schedule. However, skipping it is a false efficiency. Make the investment, and not only will you boost your ability to reliably do the things you've committed to doing, but you'll also give your mind a chance to relax and trust the process you've set up for dealing with the chaos around you. That in turn will make you more productive, and more than make up for the time you put into it.

Arrive Early and Work Late

I owe all my success in life to having been always a quarter of an hour before my time.

– Lord Nelson

This principle can be controversial. On the one hand, it's not advisable to seek a reputation solely for working more hours. Just because your boss works out at 4:00 a.m. and is in the office by 5:30 a.m. doesn't mean that you suddenly need to wake up hours before dawn and find someone else to drop the kids off at school. Set a schedule that works for you, make sure your manager approves it, and you'll be fine.

That said, it's also true that getting in early and staying late, at least occasionally, can yield some material advantages. It doesn't take too many early mornings to gain a reputation for coming in early. If you start out right away by showing up in the office early, you'll gain a reputation that's likely to stick even if you're not actually there every morning.

It's usually better to be in early as opposed to staying late. It will give you time to focus on completing something challenging with minimal distraction, while your mind is still clear. Mornings are the best time to tackle the most dreaded thing on your to-do list. If you check off just one, as the first thing you do each morning, you'll keep your list manageable and have one less thing to worry about throughout the day.

If you decide to stay late, Thursdays are a great day to clear your inbox as you head into Friday, and subsequently the weekend. It's a great feeling to know that you have things under control as you walk out of the office on Friday.

Of course, you don't always have to stay in the office to show that you're willing to work late. When used sparingly, an effective means of showing that you're willing to work late is to hold your deliverable and send it out from home in the evening. Finish it during the day and then head home, go for a jog, get some dinner, watch TV and then quickly review it before hitting send. The next day people will say, "Wow, I can't believe you were up until 10:00 last night working on that." Tell them that you finished most of it during the day but wanted to review it before sending it out. They won't believe you, which in this case is a good thing.

Under no circumstances should you feel compelled to put a tracking device on your boss's car so that you can beat him to the office, and stay until he leaves in the evening. It's important that you set your own schedule and stick to it as best you can. However, being flexible and putting in extra time when required can help you get more done and also help you gain a reputation for being a committed and dependable worker.

Stay Positive

Those who say it cannot be done should not interrupt those doing it.

– Chinese Proverb

Strive to maintain a positive attitude every day, in every interaction, with every person you encounter. Being positive does not mean ignoring or discounting the issues at hand. On the contrary, to be truly positive you must be willing to acknowledge problems, face them head-on, and offer solutions. Anyone can be positive when things are going great. Leaders find ways to positively influence even the toughest situations.

Being positive starts with being positive about yourself. Don't belittle yourself in an attempt to gain favor or compliment. If someone does compliment your work, say thank you. But avoid the temptation to constantly seek the praise of others. If you do great work, praise will find you.

Secondly, maintain a positive attitude regarding your coworkers. It's easy to be positive about the people who take their work seriously and treat you with respect. In order to maintain a positive outlook, which is critical to your own success and well-being, find a way to be positive about everyone with whom you work.

It will inevitably seem unfair that some people can get away with doing less, or with circumventing the rules that everyone else has to follow. It can be tempting to throw someone under the bus, for the sake of the team if not solely for yourself. But doing so will only pull you toward the dark side. Stay positive and let the bus find them.

For those who mean well, but just don't seem to have what it takes, help them as best you can. Everyone has something to offer. You may be surprised what you can learn from those who seem least capable of offering insight. And you may find that they have an influence over your career that you had previously overlooked. Go out of your way to find people who need your help, even if you don't think anyone will ever know.

Be generous in acknowledging help from others. If you really did something all by yourself, consider if it would have been better if you had involved others. Even if something has been assigned solely to you, it can be helpful to pull in others for advice on how to get started and for feedback on the finished product.

One way to stay positive is to maintain a strong focus on the present. The past cannot be changed and the future cannot be hastened. Focus on what you can do, right now, to make things better.

It can be tempting to match the tone of the negative voices around you. Leaders stay above the fray and maintain a positive outlook. The person most likely to be chosen to lead is the one who believes that it can be done.

Set Your Own Goals

I always wanted to be somebody, but now I realize I should have been more specific.

– Lily Tomlin

You may be able to scrape by for years without setting any goals. There are typically more things to do than people to do them, which can provide you with a steady stream of work starting now and ending at retirement. The problem with this approach is that a pseudo-random amalgam of people will have determined the course of your forty-year career, with only passive involvement from yourself.

You can significantly advance your career by setting your own goals and working toward them. It's surprising how many people essentially let someone else set goals for them. While that approach requires less effort and makes complaining easier, you're going to have to set your own goals if you want to accomplish something meaningful over the course of your career.

Like many topics in this book, there is a wealth of literature covering the subject of how to set and attain goals. But even spending too much time reading about how to set goals can be a distraction from actually making them and then working to achieve them. Sometimes it's best just to get started.

To that end, here are four basic steps you should consider when defining career goals. These apply to anything you want to accomplish throughout the course of your career and generally apply to just about anything else you wish to accomplish, even if not directly related to work.

The first step is to define what you want to achieve. This can be difficult, especially if defining a longer-term goal such as the proverbial "Where do you want to be in five years?" It's OK if you don't have a long-term career goal. Many people don't. However, it's a good idea to have a goal that, at a minimum, covers the transition from your current role into your next one. That's a reasonable horizon.

It can take serious effort to understand what your options are, and how best to balance what you want to do with what you'll be successful doing. Talk with people that you trust and get their input. Don't worry about appearing restless in your current role. Just let people know that you're trying to plan ahead and have a longer-term view in mind.

Once you determine your desired outcome, or at least narrow it down to a couple of options, the second step is to list a few concrete things that you can do to make progress toward your goal. For professional goals this might be getting exposure to a new part of the business or learning a new skill. Keep at it until you can write down some specific steps that will get you closer to your goal. You don't need to know how to achieve it completely, just how to get closer to it. Think about how to use the things you do at work every day to get you closer to your long-term goals.

Next, tell others about your goals. Tell people who can help you map out the next steps toward your goal. Also tell people who can provide assistance and encouragement. Involving others is a key step in moving something from just an idea to an actual objective.

Finally, find a suitable method to track your progress and set aside time to do it on a regular basis. There are many ways to do this, but few work better than an index card and a pencil. The key is consistency, not technique.

You might choose to focus on goals related to your personal life, your career, learning something new, or accomplishing something for someone else. You might choose to only set goals thirty days in advance, or you might set a goal that will take decades to achieve. Ultimately it's up to you, however the more you can crystalize the vision of what you want to accomplish, the more people will be excited to help. Hopefully you'll also be excited about the progress you're making toward your goals, which will make what you do on a daily basis more fulfilling, even if the substance of it hasn't fundamentally changed. Goals can add positive context to the things you're already doing.

One final note about setting goals. Don't hesitate to make a really big long-term goal that you have no idea how to accomplish. It might take you a long time to chip away at it, and you may even change it significantly over time. But there is an almost tangible energy that comes from setting a big goal.

Figure out what that is and find a way to get started. You won't regret it.

Meet With Your Manager

I want to share something with you: The three little sentences that will get you through life. Number 1: Cover for me. Number 2: Oh, good idea, Boss! Number 3: It was like that when I got here.

– Homer Simpson

It's important to have regular one-on-one meetings with your manager. If you don't have anything scheduled, you should ask if it's OK to set up a recurring meeting. Weekly is best, but once every two weeks is the minimum. It's important to have this time even if you talk casually on a regular basis, since it's a good forum for you to get structured feedback and direction.

Understand that your manager is going to be very busy. This might be a result of legitimate business activities, or it might be something less critical such as fantasy football. Regardless, most managers find ways to keep busy and resent suggestions to the contrary. It's essential that you respect the time you have together and use it as efficiently as possible.

The best approach for a weekly meeting is to provide a written summary. This could be a simple list of discussion points, or a list of projects with status and some callouts on where you need help. Your list should always be in priority order, since you might not have time to cover everything. Creating a written agenda is a great approach for any meeting, especially when you need to take control but you're not the one in charge. Having an agenda also shows your boss that you know what you're working on, leaving him less likely to try to give you additional work to fill a perceived void.

If you're not able to meet, send the same agenda with some brief notes and offer to answer any questions. Don't express frustration if your manager isn't able to meet with you.

Every manager has a different style and will want to be informed and involved in a different way. Ask for feedback to make sure you're communicating at the right frequency and level of detail.

Remain Neutral

I dream of a better tomorrow, when chickens can cross the road and not be questioned about their motives.

– Anonymous

Sometimes wars break out. No one plans on having a war. It usually starts with a disagreement, gets fueled by mistrust and poor communication, and eventually heads toward mutually assured destruction.

Wars can serve to break up the monotony of day-to-day office life. The best wars are full of secret maneuvers, covert communiqués and secret hand signals. But they can also severely damage your career.

For this reason you must avoid taking sides at all cost. This is sound advice for anyone, but it's critical if you're in an entry-level role because you haven't had a chance yet to build a network of people who can protect you when things go bad. And as exciting as these skirmishes may seem, they almost always end badly for someone. In fact it's difficult to think of a scenario where a war like this might have a positive impact on your career. At best it has no impact, and at worst it can be devastating.

You should avoid even the appearance of taking sides. Once we were in the middle of a major intraoffice battle. We're talking Godfather style, go to the mattresses kind of war. On one side were the veterans of the company, having spent the better part of a decade working toward its success. On the other side was a newcomer, suspected to have been secretly assigned to ferret out problems and report back to our holding company's senior management.

She asked to meet with me. I thought I was being discrete but someone saw me leave the building and get into her car as we went to lunch one day. I lost the trust of colleagues I had worked very hard to build. I hadn't done anything wrong, but I was accused of "sleeping with the enemy" and marked as a traitor to the cause.

The question of whether or not I did anything truly wrong is not the point. I got involved in something that was too big for me to handle. In the end my boss had to use some of his political capital to bail me out. Luckily he was willing to do so, or – as crazy as it may sound – I would likely have had to look for a job someplace else.

Whether it's an all-out war, or just a minor scuffle, stay away from office politics whenever you can. Neutrality is not weakness. Switzerland ranks in the top five countries for per capita gun ownership, and they're trained to use them. Stay sharp, be aware and defend your neutrality at all costs.

Know When to Walk Away

Do not argue with an idiot. He will drag you down to his level and beat you with experience.

– Greg King

At some point, something will happen at work that will make you really angry. Oddly enough it's often the smallest injustices that hit a nerve and get us fired up.

A number of years ago I was working with a close friend on a big upgrade to an internal company web site. It had been neglected for a long time, and we had volunteered to make it better. We worked really hard and were proud of our work. When it came time for the unveiling, we just needed one thing: a domain name. Having been previously hosted at some impossible-to-remember jumble of dots and slashes, we wanted something simple and easy to remember. It seemed like a reasonable request, especially given how much effort we had invested.

The response to our request quite literally said that we were not important enough to have a domain name, that it would never be granted, and that we had wasted company resources by submitting the request.

I was mad. My friend was livid. He crafted an email to our superiors with an opening salvo I still remember word for word. It read, "This decision reeks of corporate bureaucracy." Indeed it did, but fortunately he asked me to read the email before he sent it, and we both eventually concluded that deleting it was the wisest course of action.

The principle here is to never initiate a conversation when you're upset. If you're in the midst of a conversation and you sense that you're getting angry, ask to take a break. You're not going to accomplish anything productive when you're mad. Take a walk, drink some water, punch a wall, talk to a friend – but don't reengage until you've returned to a state of calm.

Further, never walk into your manager's office, or head over to human resources if you're upset. Wait until you can make the request in a logical, coherent way. Be extra careful with email. Its indelibility could enable a permanent record of your ill-advised communication. When in doubt, ask a friend to review your email before you send it to make sure it's appropriate.

Once I had someone very rudely demand a brand new laptop for one of his employees, because the one she was currently using was making a "funny clicking sound." He threatened to go over my head if I did not consent. I was livid. The Chief Executive Officer (CEO) sat right across the hall from me. I stormed into his office and told him what an ass this manager was being. I learned two things that day. The first was that these two men were best friends. The second was to never walk into the CEO's office without taking a moment to cool down. Luckily our CEO gave me a second chance, but it was not a career-enhancing move.

Getting upset from time to time is part of any job, and in some cases it can give you a bit of extra motivation to cover all your bases. Just be sure that you're controlling your emotions and channeling that energy toward productive activities, rather than letting your emotions control you.

Be Nice to People

I destroy my enemies when I make them my friends.

– Abraham Lincoln

Once we had a young woman come in and present a creative concept to our team. The project leader from our side was late but we decided to get started anyway. Then someone on our team started berating the work in savage fashion. He interrupted constantly and after several minutes stopped the conversation to say that the direction she was heading was not only wrong, but highly offensive and an affront to the company. Her neck started to show splotches of red and she was clearly distraught. He continued.

I was about 40 years his junior and didn't feel it was my place to tell him to stop. No one else in the room, all of whom had much more experience than I did, asked him to stop. I regret not having supported the presenter, who was clearly just trying to do her job, by asking my coworker to be quiet. It reflected poorly on our company and fifteen years later I still remember it vividly.

About ten minutes into the meeting, the project manager from our company arrived, and explained that the work was consistent with the direction she had provided. No apologies were offered.

While this is a particularly pointed example, you will most likely face a whole host of people at work who will be rude to you. You will also encounter a number of people who are friendly to you for the purpose of selling something, and it will be tempting to be rude to them, so that they will leave you alone and let you get back to work.

You will see managers at varying levels of the organization being rude to their employees, in a misplaced attempt at motivation. You may even find people being rude just for the sport of it, or in a misplaced attempt to boost their ego.

It's important to be direct, but it's never appropriate to be rude. Your goal should be to communicate clearly and honestly, while maintaining a respectful demeanor at all times.

The rules for politeness differ greatly by country and by situation. However, regardless of the circumstance, ask yourself if people will have a higher or lesser opinion of you after the conversation, and act accordingly. It's possible to communicate even the most difficult things in a way that keeps this principle in balance.

Ignoring this rule in an effort to save time, be considered more of a leader, or worst of all as an opportunity to blow off steam, will be detrimental in the long run. People move between companies. They may have personal or professional relationships that are unknown to you, and most people have a long memory for people who have offended them. Be sure you're in the business of making friends, not enemies, regardless of the message you need to deliver.

Attend Staff Meeting

Unfaithfulness in the keeping of an appointment is an act of clear dishonesty. You may as well borrow a person's money as his time.

– Horace Mann

It seems that there is always someone on every team with a recurring excuse for missing staff meeting. Usually the reasons have at least an air of legitimacy, such as an important meeting, imminent deadline, or sudden crisis that requires attention.

This is likely the most important meeting your boss convenes on a regular basis. It is her opportunity to receive input from her team and also disseminate key information. As such, failing to make it a priority is unwise. Even if your boss seems to be giving you a free pass, you'll likely miss some important information and forgo opportunities to influence others.

Beyond just showing up to the meeting, there are a couple of other things to keep in mind. First, always have a list of at least three things that have happened in your area since your last meeting, including at least one accomplishment. Whether you have a formal "roundtable" where everyone speaks in turn, or it's something that comes out naturally in the course of discussion, having these prepared will allow you to focus on being fully present in the meeting, without being preoccupied with trying to come up with what you're going to say.

Being now free to fully participate, see that you do. Ask questions and raise concerns, but never call anyone out unless you've discussed the issue with them before and have let them know that you'd like to discuss it in staff meeting. This is a place and time for making friends, not enemies.

Balance is also key for meetings of this nature. It's not a time to show off, but it is a time to talk about what's going well, and where you face challenges. It's a great time to thank your coworkers for their help, and congratulate them sincerely on their own successes. And it's a good time to listen and learn about the needs of the organization, and consider how you might better contribute.

You can use staff meetings to significantly enhance your work experience if you show up on a regular basis, take the time to prepare in advance and do your best to fully participate. If you're not having regular staff meetings, suggest a few topics to your boss and ask if she'd like to have one, and if you can help facilitate.

Be Professional

If you wouldn't write it and sign it, don't say it.
– Earl Wilson

Every office environment maintains a unique definition of what it means to be professional, and sometimes it can be hard to define. You might see a wide range of behaviors, ranging from completely buttoned up to casual, and from highly respectful to utterly derogatory.

Being professional means being formal when formality is called for. Don't call your boss "buddy." Don't ask the CEO "wassup" in the elevator. Think about the amount of formality you think is appropriate and then go one step further. This will cover you for any generational differences in communication.

Being professional also means being respectful. Refrain from using foul or coarse language when you're at work, even if other people do. Don't belittle people, even when they deserve it. Don't make jokes at the expense of others, even if they are funny.

Although your company may tolerate or even condone certain unprofessional behavior, going down that path is inadvisable, unless you intend to stay there for the rest of your career. Your next job is most likely to come via your network, which includes current coworkers and external partners, including vendors. Make sure you represent yourself in a way that when you're ready to move on, you have options outside the company. They may laugh along with you now, but when they get a big promotion to go work on Wall Street, you don't want them to think of you as the office prankster.

Staying professional through the ups and downs of your work life, in every situation, will increase the respect others have for you, and keep your options open for opportunities inside the company and beyond.

Line Up or Speak Up

If you don't like something, change it. If you can't change it, change your attitude.

– Maya Angelou

You're going to run into a lot of decisions you don't agree with. In each of these situations, you will need to decide if it's worth the effort to push back and try to change things, or simply go along with the decision even though you don't agree.

The time to raise any concerns is at the start of something. It's fine to raise legitimate issues, but once you've had the chance to do so, it becomes time to throw all of your support into the effort, regardless of whether or not you feel your concerns were addressed.

It's said that perfect is the enemy of good. You may be able to come up with plenty of legitimate reasons why something is either not the best solution, or shouldn't be done at all. It's fair game to communicate all of that in a rational, well-considered manner. However, the wrong approach is often better than no approach at all. It's also true that you may just not have all the information.

Being honest and direct when communicating your concerns will increase the trust others feel they can place in you, as long as you then yield to the final decision once it's been made. The only exception to this is when you believe there is a real question of ethics. These circumstances are rare, where you or someone acting on your behalf would be breaking a law or violating a basic moral principle. Examples of this include bribing a public official, illegal dumping, or mishandling patient health records.

If it doesn't involve breaking the law – just what you consider good judgment – you should defer to those who are in charge. In most cases they're in charge for a reason. If it turns out that they're wrong, then you will have done your job by raising your concerns and delivering on your individual assignment, and the overall results will speak for themselves. Perhaps next time someone else will be put in charge, and if that's you, then you'll want to know that others will support you and follow your lead.

Write an Elevator Speech

The human brain is a wonderful thing. It starts working the moment you are born, and never stops until you stand up to speak in public.

– George Jessel

I once worked with a colleague who walked up and down five flights of stairs at least ten times a day, not for exercise but to avoid running into senior executives in the elevator. As it turns out he had good reason to avoid them, given that a colleague of his had once been questioned in an elevator, had failed to provide an adequate response, and was fired within the hour.

While this is an extreme example, it's still critical that you have an elevator speech ready at any time. A good elevator speech succinctly explains what you do and how you add value to the company. The following is a typical exchange:

Joelle, it's nice to meet you. I'm Steven.

Hi Steven, what are you working on?

I'm a business analyst in the accounts payable department. I'm working on a project to reduce the time and costs associated with onboarding new suppliers.

That's it. That's your speech. It should be no more than 30 seconds. You might very well be working on more than one project, but for your elevator speech you should pick just one.

In general you should choose the project you know the best, rather than the one that you think will sound most impressive, since you'll need to be able to answer follow-up questions. This is known as being "three questions deep." In the example above, you might expect Joelle to ask who you're working with, when the project will be complete, or how long it currently takes to onboard a new supplier.

A good elevator speech with prepared answers to likely follow-up questions will boost your confidence when the opportunity arises to meet someone new, and will put you and your work in the best possible light.

Be Good to
Your Body

*If by gaining knowledge we destroy our health,
we labour for a thing that will be useless in our
hands.*

– John Locke

If you're young and relatively healthy, it can be easy
to ignore some basic things that will keep you fit
once the pressures of corporate life start to mount.
You might not see an impact right away, but
eventually it will catch up with you.

Having a professional job working in an office
can be more physically demanding than you might

anticipate. I've worked for thirty-six hours straight, gone for months at a time with only a couple of hours of rest each night and written off vacation time as something I could not expect to take. I have at times convinced myself that I had no time to exercise and no time to eat. I've skipped out on medical treatment and ignored signs of serious stress.

I don't regret when I've had to do this on a short-term basis. I'm willing to skip lunch every once in a while if I know I'm doing something worthwhile. However, I do regret the times when I let these behaviors develop into habits.

Taking care of yourself is not just a long-term, post-retirement proposition. It's also an essential part of ensuring that you continue to operate at a peak level. You'll receive not only the direct benefits of proper diet and exercise but also an important halo effect, namely that people are more likely to hire and promote those who look like they're in control of their own bodies. This does not mean that you need to fit any particular body type, or diet until you reach nine percent body fat. It simply means that you should endeavor to maintain a healthy, positive appearance.

Every day a candidate is passed over for a promotion because someone in leadership believes that they're not physically or emotionally able to handle it. In fact, within the fastest-paced areas of the business this can be one of the most significant factors in who gets tapped when something new comes along.

"She looks like she's about to blow a gasket," my manager would say if I proposed giving a project to someone who looked a bit frazzled. Another manager would say, "Have you looked at him? We're going to send that poor guy to the hospital if we give him something else to do." In some cases I think these employees were actually trying to convey how maxed out they were, in an effort to show their commitment and loyalty. Ironically, it was all too often the ones that were slacking off, but at least showed some amount of physical composure, that got the nod when the opportunity came.

When it comes to your health, all signs point toward taking care of yourself as the first priority. You'll be happier, more productive and more likely to be tapped for something interesting.

Follow the
Chain of Command

Painting is easy when you don't know how, but very difficult when you do.

– Edgar Degas

Nearly every company eventually develops a hierarchical bureaucracy in order to perpetuate its survival. This bureaucracy is incredibly powerful. If you truly love it, there is probably something wrong with you. You may find it to be outmoded and inefficient. But whatever you do, don't underestimate its strength. Some rules just need to be followed, at least for now. One day perhaps you'll be steering the ship, but for now just try not to get run over by it.

First, never go over someone's head without trying to resolve the problem directly first. If you cannot resolve it, the cardinal rule is that you must inform the other people affected that you're going to escalate the issue, before you do so. It is often inconvenient or uncomfortable to do this, but it is worth it. As long as you do, you will find that you'll be able to build trust even among those with whom you're struggling to resolve issues or find middle ground. If you do not do this, people will feel that you're going around them and this will ultimately make things worse, even if it ends up fixing the immediate problem.

The second, even more important rule is to never go over your manager's head. This too may be more difficult than it initially seems. Someone in your chain of command may try to extract information from you. She may lure you with tokens of power and prestige. Do not be tempted to comply. Only say positive things. If you can't think of anything positive to say, then say nothing at all. But never suppose that these senior executives can be trusted. In the end, you will be the one who gets hurt, not your manager.

They've all been around longer, and know how to play the game.

Talk with your manager and ask what's OK to share and what's not. Some things, even if generally positive, should be communicated by him and not by you. For example, let's say you're working on a research project that has a high chance of failure, but a huge payoff if it turns out to be successful. Letting the cat out of the bag too soon will result in the senior executive getting excited about the possibilities. Initially you feel energized to be working on something of interest to senior management. But by catching their attention, suddenly the project becomes a must-do for the company – despite that fact that it never had much of a chance for success in the first place. If you do complete it, you've only just met expectations. If you don't, then you've failed. It might have been better to keep the project under wraps and let your manager figure out the right time to make it public. In other words, some things need to stay within your team.

Early in my career I came to know someone on the senior leadership team at our company, and he asked to meet with me on a weekly basis. He was very cordial and laid back. During the first meeting he said he just wanted to know what I was working on, so that he could help in any way possible. I told him what I was working on. It seemed like a good meeting and I was happy to have the exposure. Before I could even walk back to my desk, he had called my manager and lambasted him for not saying anything about a couple of topics I was exploring at the time. From then on I always sent my boss a quick list of the things I was working on prior to my check-in with his boss. He would usually cross one or two things off the list. Everything went fine after that.

Lastly, be aware of any warring factions that might impact your team. It's quite common for leaders to have intracompany rivals. These are people they distrust, who in their eyes are always looking for some way to make them look bad. Even if you don't believe this to actually be the case, be especially careful in your associations with these rival leaders. At best it can make your life unnecessarily difficult. If you think all of this sounds crazy, and that your company is not like this, then you're not looking hard enough.

Once I had a manager who, as soon as she heard someone else in the company was working on something, would say that her team had been working on that as well, and that it was close to being completed. It was her attempt to steal some thunder from her rivals. The problem was that in virtually every case we were not actually working on whatever she said we were working on. She would come back from staff meeting and get the team together. "OK, we have two weeks to develop a prototype of a customer order entry system." We knew the other team had been working on this for months. It was a recipe for failure. In cases like this the smart ones on the team politely explained why they were too busy to take on the project. But usually there was someone who volunteered, lured by the idea of pulling off a major win for the company in only two weeks time. They inevitably got burned in the process.

To summarize, you might not like the politics inherent in your company's culture. You may wisely choose not to participate, to the extent that's possible. But ignoring politics completely and skirting the established chain of command will only draw you in further, not exempt you from its influence.

Be Neat

You could eat sushi off my bookshelf. My cleaning regime is like a battleground. I'm Genghis Khan and my cleaning products are my Mongolian army and I take no prisoners. The rest of my life is an experiment in chaos so I like to keep my flat neat.

– Ryan Adams

I once worked for someone whose sprawling desk was topped by a mound of paper so enormous that when someone heavy walked by, the shaking would cause papers to slide off the desk and onto the floor. Just prior to a scheduled visit by some out-of-town higher-ups, he was directed in no uncertain terms that he must clear his desk, which completely ruined what in his mind was the perfect filing system. Notably, he was one of the few people I've worked with who could probably have gotten away with a desk that messy; he was a bona fide genius, having earlier in his career invented a bit of consumer technology that is now present in virtually every American home. Unless you can make a similar claim, you need to keep your desk neat.

Your desk doesn't need to be completely vacant – in fact it should not be. You should always have a few things laid out to make sure it looks like you're working on something. Trying to make it look like you're engrossed in something is not deceitful, as long as it reflects reality.

Your desk is often one of the first things people notice when being introduced to you. Make sure your desk is clean, in addition to being neat and organized. In the old days people came around at night and actually cleaned. It's much less common today, but that doesn't give you an excuse to have dust bunnies blowing around your cubicle.

Harboring a few personal mementos is OK, but you don't want someone walking past your desk to feel like they've stumbled on a shrine to your favorite sports team, or been trapped inside a giant family photo album. Limit yourself to a handful of tasteful items.

It can be helpful to have one or two things around your workspace that will help people get to know you, as long as you don't overdo it. Pick something that's indicative of a favorite hobby or activity – something you want people to ask you about.

The key is to look objectively at your workspace and make sure it reflects the image you wish to portray. You may wish to keep it sparse to indicate that you're ready to move to another assignment at any time. You may wish to have a few strategically placed stacks of paper to show that you've settled in and are knee-deep in an important project. Once you settle on a comfortable configuration, reserve a moment at the end of each day, or perhaps during a conference call, to make sure your workspace continues to project your intended message.

Keep Your Mouth Shut

If A is a success in life, then A equals x plus y plus z. Work is x; y is play; and z is keeping your mouth shut.

– Albert Einstein

There are lots of times when the best thing to say is nothing at all. When you know something that reflects negatively on someone else, don't share it unless there is a legitimate business reason to do so. Even then, be careful about how you communicate it.

Always anticipate the next question – what will the person you report this to ask or do next?

Consider the possibility that your report will not be kept in confidence. In other words, everyone will know that it was you that went and told someone.

Further, you should be prepared for a thorough cross-examination on the subject. You may be asked questions that probe deeper than you would prefer. Once you raise the issue, however, you may have little choice but to tell more than you originally anticipated. If the exploration goes deep enough, eventually it's possible to get to something you did wrong, or at best could have done differently. All of this puts your credibility at risk, so be sure it's worth taking that chance.

In short you'll be better served by being known as someone who doesn't give out secrets, rather than someone who always has the inside angle. Of course, if it involves illegal or unethical behavior, puts people in danger, or is otherwise just plain wrong, then the right thing to do is to report it. But don't try to convince yourself that you're being a whistleblower by letting your boss know that your coworker shows up late on Thursdays. It's not worth it, and most likely she already knows.

Similarly, don't share confidential information unless it's required, even within your own company. When working with other companies, only share what's needed based on the work you're doing together. Legal departments often institute non-disclosure agreements to protect confidentiality, but in practice they do little to keep a lid on information once shared.

Another area where it's usually best to keep your mouth shut is when you're inclined to report a problem without proposing a solution. It makes you look like a complainer, even if you're saying it in the nicest possible way.

Never talk about your salary or someone else's. Doing so accomplishes very little and is almost always considered inappropriate. Don't go into detail about your health. No one wants to know the details of your bodily functions, even if they appear to take interest for the sake of politeness. Refrain from boasting too much about the last place you worked. If it was that great, you should have stayed there.

A favorite executive trick is to be disarmingly informal and friendly, in an effort to get information from you that you know better than to disclose. Be on the lookout for this at all times. As an entry-level employee, you hold tremendous insight into how the organization is functioning. That's good, and you'll no doubt have valuable information to share. However, you also hold a treasure chest of information including how your boss is truly performing, what people say about the executive team when they're not around, and all sorts of other anecdotes that you should never disclose. Never trade information that should be kept confidential for what appears to be a closer relationship with a coworker.

Finally, be careful about making commitments on behalf of other people. A primary reason entry-level employees don't get invited to meetings is because their managers are afraid they will say something that oversteps their bounds. They're afraid you'll say, "Oh, it's not that hard" when they know how much work will actually be required to satisfy their boss. It's never inappropriate to say that you need to check with your manager first before committing to something.

By knowing when to keep your mouth shut, you'll maximize the opportunity to be heard when you do have something productive to say.

Get Enough Sleep

Each night, when I go to sleep, I die. And the next morning, when I wake up, I am reborn.

– Mahatma Gandhi

I'd been working on a big project for several months, and sleep was in short supply. It was the night before our first demo and it was getting late. Knowing it would take well into the early morning hours to get everything in order, I turned to our executive sponsor and said, "I've got this, if you want to go home and get some sleep before your big meeting tomorrow." After all, he would be meeting with the CEO of one of the largest companies in the world in about six hours, and the fate of our entire group was hanging in the balance. "Sleep is for the weak" was his curt response.

I've worked with countless people that ignore the need for sleep, and even view sleep deprivation as a badge of honor. People compete for how little sleep they can chalk up, as a measure of how hard they're working, and as a gauge of general toughness.

You will perform better with sleep. You're likely to live longer. You'll be happier, and you'll make better decisions. Take the long view and treat sleep like the medical and professional necessity that it is.

Businesses do not "run on caffeine." You may hear that your industry, whether it's software development, or banking or entertainment, is different. In fact, they're all the same. These businesses run in spite of the fact that so many get so little sleep, not because of it. Try it yourself and you will see the difference.

Of course, there are times when you just can't get the sleep you'd like to, whether that's because you're a new parent, you're jetlagged, or just stressed from people trying to get you to work eighteen hours a day. But let this be the exception rather than the rule. If it becomes a chronic issue, you will chronically underperform relative to your potential.

Strive to be the one person in the room with enough sleep, and you'll be the one they all look to for direction through their haze of sleep deprivation.

Pay Attention to Details

Be faithful in small things because it is in them that your strength lies.

- Attributed to Mother Teresa

Get in the habit of looking at every detail. It's better to be slow or to ask too many questions than to gloss over something that might be important.

When someone hands you a business card, pay attention to everything that's written on it. Ask about what they do or where they're from. Right from your first introduction you'll be showing that you're someone who pays attention to the details.

If someone mentions something you're not familiar with, ask. If the occasion doesn't permit questions, for whatever reason, make a list for yourself and follow up later. Do your own research and then ask questions to fill in the gaps.

If presented with something that appears opaque on the surface, think about ways to get into the details. Ask for documentation and assemble a list of questions as you read it. Pull together a meeting with the architects of whatever you're working on and ask them to walk you through the process or system using a diagram if available, or even just a whiteboard. If there isn't much documentation, or it's out-of-date or obtuse, start to assemble your own based on what you know, and ask others to validate it. That will force you to develop a detailed understanding of the subject.

Another great way to pay attention to details is to start collecting data. Pull every kind of data you can and do some analysis. Keep digging. Keep asking questions. Before long you'll be knee-deep in the details. Don't worry about giving up your strategic viewpoint. Usually when people complain about others being in the weeds, they're just trying to mask their lack of knowledge on a particular topic.

Focusing on risks is also a good way to cut through the fluff and get down to what matters. Ask people how, why or when something is likely to fail. That immediately pulls you into a level where you have to focus on specifics. Everything works great in theory. Ask about how things work in practice.

Take small projects and minor responsibilities seriously. If you can't be trusted to do something like fill out a time card or reconcile your expenses, then no one will trust you to handle more significant responsibilities or manage larger budgets.

The ancient Greek philosopher Heraclitus said "men who wish to know about the world must learn about it in its particular details." Not much has changed in this regard in the last 2,500 years.

Stay Sober

You only have to do a very few things right in your life so long as you don't do too many things wrong.

– Warren Buffett

Some professions would seem to require a lot of drinking. Everywhere I've worked I've heard someone recount an epic tale about salespeople closing a massive deal by drinking their counterparts under the table. I have personally witnessed countless dinners, office parties and conferences where alcohol was abused on a massive scale.

I have worked with too many people who became famous not for their expertise or job performance, but for drinking too much at social functions, and then doing outrageous things. They probably knew that they drank a little too much, but everyone seemed to enjoy it and no one told them to stop. No one goes to a demolition derby and asks the drivers to drive a little slower. These displays of public drunkenness often seem amusing at the start, but can end in disaster.

In fact, during the very first week of my first corporate job, I was sent off to training with the other new employees. We had all recently graduated from school and had managed to be hired by a well-respected company. Many had flown to the US from Europe or Asia to be at this training center. That weekend about a dozen people decided to throw a party, complete with a bathtub full of beer, in one of the on-site hotel rooms. Someone complained about the noise, the training program administrators were notified, and a number of people were fired the next day.

Far from being a prohibitionist, I would simply offer a word of caution. Know your limits, and if for some unadvisable reason you choose to ignore them, do it on your own time. A free drink can cost you a great deal.

Don't succumb to peer pressure to drink more than you know you should, or at all if that's your decision. Being the one person who's sober can be a remarkable advantage. You're much more likely to learn – and remember – things you might not otherwise learn, and keep under wraps things you might otherwise divulge.

Having a drink with someone to forge a relationship, celebrate a success or stay in touch can be an effective business tool. But anything beyond that should be done on your own time, far away from the office. Risking a reputation as a teetotaler is better than overdoing it and forging a reputation that can be difficult, if not impossible, to change.

Memorize the Mission

You can claim to be surprised once; after that you are unprepared.

– Ray Charles

There are some things about your company that you'll be expected to know, even if you don't think they're relevant. Senior executives spend a lot of time trying to craft things like mission statements, and while they arguably do very little in terms of actually impacting most companies, their creators would like to think otherwise. Therefore, when someone quizzes you, as will almost certainly happen at some point, you need to be ready.

In addition to mission statements, you should pay special attention to outputs from Human Resources, which often take the form of values or behaviors. Don't be surprised if someone asks you a question such as which of your company's five core values you're most aligned with. They're checking to see if you're paying attention, and if you're willing to work within the system.

If your CEO sends a list of key initiatives for the year, print it out and memorize it. If you're expected to know them, then you'll avoid embarrassment. If you're not expected to know them, then people will be surprised and impressed when you show that you're capable of and interested in thinking about the bigger picture.

Dress Appropriately

The apparel oft proclaims the man.
– William Shakespeare, Hamlet

Every workplace is a little different when it comes to attire. You might work at a bank in New York City where three-piece suits, designer dresses and expensive shoes are the norm, or you might work at a startup in San Francisco where dressing up means putting on your best t-shirt.

The key is to understand the expectation and fit somewhere within it. One of the things managers dread the most is talking to their employees about how they're dressed. As a result, many things go unsaid even though they are certainly not unnoticed.

Regardless of your office environment, you need to look the part. If you're underdressed, your manager may hesitate to put you in front of senior leadership or key customers. If you're overdressed, people may feel you're either trying too hard or angling for some kind of undue promotion.

Pay attention to details – hair, nails, belt, shoes. Treat every day like it's an interview. When moving between roles within a company, you've likely either passed or failed well before the official interview takes place. Never let a hole in your sock be the thing that keeps you from the job you've always wanted.

To that end, it's never a bad idea to keep a change of clothes at the office. That way if someone bumps into you in the lunchroom and you find yourself covered in berry yogurt, you can just quickly change your clothes instead of trying to explain why you smell like a dairy product. Always be ready to meet with anyone at any time. You never know when an opportunity will present itself, and the best opportunities don't always provide advance notice.

Be the Bearer of
Bad News

*Good night, Westley. Good work. Sleep well. I'll
most likely kill you in the morning.*

– William Goldman, The Princess Bride

Douglas Adams wrote "nothing travels faster than
the speed of light with the possible exception of bad
news." There is usually only a very small window in
which to perform damage control once something
bad happens.

The best scenario, other than avoiding the
unfortunate situation altogether of course, is to
provide some warning ahead of time. Signaling your

concern, or raising a possible risk, is always better than having something happen out of the blue. It shows that you're paying attention and trying to think strategically. Even raising the concern just prior to the problem occurring is better than communicating that something unexpected and terrible has, in fact, just happened.

For those times when you can't provide advance warning, it is imperative that you act quickly. Don't wait for someone else to communicate the news to anyone who might be impacted. If it's your area of responsibility, you should be the one to let people know.

Your first course of action should be to notify your manager. She needs to feel engaged and informed, since she's the most likely person to be contacted if it's a serious problem.

Your second action, assuming your manager doesn't feel the need to manage the issue directly, is to send a communication to those impacted. If you don't have all the details yet, just send out a note saying that there appears to be an issue, that you're working on it, and that you'll provide an update shortly. That will at least stop the mass hysteria caused by people wondering if other people know it's a problem, and it establishes you as the point of contact.

For problems that take a while to solve, provide updates on a regular basis. If it's truly urgent, such as a system being down, you may need to send an update as often as every fifteen minutes. If it's less urgent then perhaps a daily email would be more appropriate, until the issue is resolved. Never leave anyone wondering if you're still paying attention to the problem.

When you do have a final resolution, send a recap and hold a meeting if necessary to review. The recap should clearly describe the problem, the actions or conditions that caused it, the business impact, the steps taken to resolve the issue, and follow-ups required to ensure that the problem does not happen again.

Bad things happen all the time. By taking ownership of problems when they occur, people will learn they can trust you to manage a crisis and will develop confidence in your ability to reduce the likelihood of future problems.

Write Things Down

History will be kind to me for I intend to write it.

– Winston Churchill

One of the best things you can do while trying to figure out how things work is to create a document. You're likely to find a lot of people with some knowledge about how things work, but in most companies it's a rare day that you're able to find an accurate, up-to-date document on a given topic. Time spent mapping out processes or systems, or constructing a timeline of events, will not only give you a better understanding of how things work, but will add value to your team. People are also more likely to give you information if they know they'll be getting some kind of documentation in return.

For work that you initiate, make sure you document it comprehensively. If no standard exists for this, create one. Pay attention to everything, including grammar, spelling, layout and fonts. Make it look great and it will last a very long time. Put your name and contact information on it.

Finally, when someone asks you to do something, make sure you write that down also. Even if you can remember it, you should still write it down. It gives people a sense of confidence, knowing that you've captured the request.

For anything more than a casual inquiry, it's a great practice to send an email with the details of the request, just to make sure everything is correct. You might be confident that you understood it correctly, but sending it in an email gives requestors a chance to review it and make sure they didn't miss anything. It also gives you a virtual paper trail in case you need to refer back to the email to show that you met the objective.

While using a laptop or tablet to capture notes is often more efficient, depending on your company culture it might be best to take notes on paper first.

Doing so gives your coworkers confidence that you're paying attention, and not checking your email or being otherwise distracted. If you choose to use paper, invest in a high-quality bound notebook. People feel great when they see that you're writing down information they've given you into something that looks permanent and professional.

Avoid Acronyms

Style is a simple way of saying complicated things.

– Jean Cocteau

Businesses love acronyms. Some may be familiar to you, while others will undoubtedly be new. Some will be general industry terms, while others may be specific to your line of work.

Do your best to quickly learn the acronyms used at your company. Ask for a glossary, and if one doesn't exist, offer to create one. That way you will be adding value to the organization, while learning yourself.

Once you have learned the company's acronyms, use them as little as possible. If you must use them in writing, always define them first, like this:

The next version of our Computer Aided Drawing (CAD) software will support three-dimensional renderings.

If you must use acronyms while speaking, define the acronym first, even when speaking to people that you believe already know them. This is especially relevant when talking to senior executives. Even if they know the jargon – which they may not – they'll want to know they can put you in front of customers. In these situations, don't be surprised if you get asked about a very basic acronym. They may simply be testing you to see if you can speak like a human.

It may be tempting to use as many acronyms as possible, so that you sound more like an "old-timer." Avoid the temptation. Let them learn to talk more like you.

Use Email Wisely

Je n'ai fait celle-ci plus longue que parce que je n'ai pas eu le loisir de la faire plus courte.

I have made this longer than usual because I have not had time to make it shorter.

- Blaise Pascal

In most companies, email is the dominant form of communication. Despite efforts to get people away from their keyboards and into face-to-face meetings and phone or video chats, it's likely to remain ubiquitous for at least a good portion of your career. Consequently, to be most effective at work, you need to be smart about how you use email.

As a general rule, emails should be concise. Most well-written emails follow a three paragraph pattern: some background or introduction to the topic, a specific request or set of actions to be performed, and then a statement concerning follow-up or next steps. As an example, an email might briefly summarize product quality issues experienced in the last thirty days, outline three specific actions to be performed, and then indicate that a meeting to review the results will be scheduled for the following week. If your email requires more than three paragraphs, most likely another medium – such as an actual document, or a meeting – is more appropriate.

Never use email to raise sensitive topics or express anger. There are better ways to do this, and the permanence of email means that it's hard to retract something you wish you hadn't said.

The email feature most likely to get you into trouble is blind carbon copy, or BCC. I've often heard coworkers rejoice when they discover that they can secretly copy someone on an email. For some reason it conjures up all sorts of nefarious possibilities.

Using BCC is dangerous, because the person receiving the blind copy may inadvertently (or intentionally) respond, revealing the BCC and making you look like you were hiding something. It's better to just send the email to its public recipients, and then forward a copy to someone else if you need to.

The best use for BCC is to send an announcement to a large group, where you want to discourage Reply to All. With BCC, they'll only be able to respond to you, which is usually a good thing if there are more than a couple dozen recipients. This eliminates the possibility of your coworkers replying to all with a comment that's inappropriate, or with a question or statement designed to cast doubt on your credibility. It also avoids the possibility of endless replies to the group saying "take me off your list," which only entices others to pile on, inevitably leading to chaos. With BCC, the only address they'll see is yours.

Your email system may have a message recall function. Don't use it. It rarely works, and only draws attention to your blunder. Simply follow up with a correction if needed. Also, some email systems allow for read receipts to let you know when someone has read your email. Don't use them. It's creepy, and gives the appearance that you have nothing better to do than track when others are reading their email.

An email feature that you should use is the automatic outgoing signature, which allows you to append a few lines of text below each message. Include your phone number in your signature, so that people can easily pick up the phone and call you if a conversation is warranted. Avoid long signatures with pictures, motivational quotes or other irrelevant information.

Make sure you always take a moment to read through an email before sending to ensure that it's clear and concise, is being sent to the right recipients, and that your spelling and grammar are correct. If you're sending an email to a large group or to someone of greater-than-average importance, take a little extra time to proofread. If you have any question about whether something is appropriate, ask someone else to give it a once-over before sending it.

The rule of thumb I was taught, as a measure of appropriateness for all email, is what is known as the *New York Times* test. If you'd be embarrassed in any way to have the contents of your email printed on the front page of the *Times*, don't send it. This is a strict standard to be sure, but the only one I know of that covers every possible circumstance.

Don't sign your name with your initials, or even worse, a single initial. There is often an unwritten rule that only senior executives sign their emails with their initials, as odd as that may sound. It's unlikely that someone will tell you not to do it, but it's still something to avoid especially when you're just starting out.

Never type in all caps and avoid crazy colors, large type, script fonts, custom backgrounds and repeated exclamation or question marks. It will get you noticed, but for the wrong reason.

Finally, switch off your email from time to time. Disable the automatic email notification that comes standard on Microsoft Outlook and most other email clients. Email is not meant to be a real-time communication protocol, and it can easily sap your productivity. It's better to set aside time throughout the day to respond to email, or respond when you have a minute between meetings. It's not easy to find blocks of time to focus on more strategic priorities, so it's important to minimize interruptions when you do have that time.

The one exception to the notification rule is that if you can set up a VIP rule, such as what's available on iOS and Android, then you should set one for your boss and other important people. With this setting enabled you'll get notified right away when these select people send you an email; the others you can deal with on your own schedule.

Given the amount of time you're likely to spend over the coming years writing, reading and responding to email, it's well worth establishing some good habits upfront.

Focus on Follow-up

Injustice is relatively easy to bear; what stings is justice.

– H. L. Mencken

On several occasions I have witnessed long-time company veterans who, while professing to be in solid command of their organizations, were scared out of their wits by relatively inexperienced and mild-mannered employees, simply because these new-comers had mastered the principle of follow-up.

When you develop a reputation for gathering action items and methodically tracking them to completion, you gain a power that is difficult to evade.

First, the basics. Following up means a laser-like focus on the take-aways from each meeting or interaction. Never let meetings adjourn without someone recapping what will happen next, even if it's not your meeting. If you're vastly junior compared to everyone else, it's OK to say something disarming like "May I just ensure I understand the action items from this meeting?"

When capturing action items from your own meetings, focus on three things: the expected outcome, due date and the person responsible. It's common for people to insist on an activity as opposed to an outcome. An example of an activity is "meet and talk about first quarter sales projections." The related outcome is "determine first quarter sales forecast." There is a big difference, and it's important to capture the outcome, not the activity.

People often evade due dates by saying that they'll complete something ASAP, or "as soon as schedules allow." If you're getting this and can't get them to give you a date, try setting a target date and say you'll check in at that point. That is more likely to prompt action.

In terms of people assigned, it's common to hear someone say, "You know what, put us all down – we all have to work on this." It's not always possible, but whenever you can you should designate one person to be the lead. If two people are responsible for something, no one is.

You should begin every meeting you lead by reviewing the list of action items from the previous meeting, and asking for a status. This is where you need to be careful, however. This principle can be so powerful, and is so infrequently applied with consistency, that you can easily wind up embarrassing people or making them feel caught off guard. Use this to your advantage when you need to, but always make sure to cover your bases by sending out a list of action items after each meeting. When possible, also send out a note a day or two prior to the next meeting to give people a moment to prepare, especially if there has been a long gap between meetings.

Finally, make sure you follow up any time you stop working on something. Perhaps someone asked you to do something, but then your boss told you not to. Even if you're quite certain that it's been communicated, it's a good idea to send an email confirming this. This also helps clarify that it wasn't your idea to stop working on it, and provides written evidence that you're no longer committed to the task. You might say something like:

Anne,

I believe you already discussed this with Steve, but I just wanted to make sure. He asked me to hold off on creating the in-depth market study until we have the consumer test results back. I'd be happy to pick it up at that point.

Roger

Following up is about making sure that people know you're committed to completing the things you've promised to do, and holding others accountable for the things they have promised to do. Many successful careers have been cemented by mastering just this one principle.

Be Responsive

*I am a man of fixed and unbending principles,
the first of which is to be flexible at all times.*

– Everett Dirksen

Being responsive means reacting quickly. In investment banking, where seconds can mean the difference between profit and loss, you might need to respond immediately to requests on a regular basis. In most circumstances that kind of responsiveness is not required. However, regardless of the industry, most businesses are cyclical in nature, meaning that you may need to step up your game at certain times, such as during a peak selling period, during annual planning or at the end of a quarter.

Note that responding quickly doesn't necessarily mean working faster. For example, if you're in a fast-response work environment you may need to respond with an email saying "I'm on it" just to let people know that you've got the request. Provide an expected completion date and ask them to call your cell phone if they need it sooner. Asking them to call your mobile phone shows that you're willing to be extra responsive, but forces the requestor to think about whether or not that level of urgency is really required. In most circumstances they will not call, but they'll appreciate the offer just the same.

It's OK to set different levels of responsiveness depending on who's contacting you. Most mobile devices allow messages from only those you specify to trigger a notification, while keeping others silent. This is a good way to make sure you're responding to your boss quickly without having your phone buzz every ten seconds.

Outside of peak periods, it's best to be consistent in your timing. If you respond to every email you get within five minutes, then most likely you won't have any uninterrupted time to think strategically. Further, if you make a habit of responding to emails within a few minutes, but then suddenly go a day without responding, people will think something is wrong. If people know you generally respond to emails within a day, they'll know to expect that and will be less likely to harass you when you don't respond right away.

Some people consider it a badge of courage to be so overwhelmed by email and phone messages that they can't possibly respond. Others just choose not to respond if they don't have time to complete a request, or if they don't consider the request to be worth the time they have. These are bad habits. Great leaders are responsive.

Your answer may not be what people are looking for, but a polite message saying you don't have time to work on something, and perhaps suggesting an alternate person or solution, is vastly better than no response. Being responsive will help you earn a reputation as a reliable leader who is able to keep things balanced and in control.

Build a Personal Brand

Our names are labels, plainly printed on the bottled essence of our past behavior.

– Logan Pearsall Smith

If you think about a company that has a strong brand, you could probably look at a piece of marketing and tell if that company produced it, based solely on its aesthetics – even if all references to the actual company or its products were removed.

When someone examines your work, even if they don't see a name attached, do they have a similar impression? Will someone be able to pick your work out of a lineup? This is a worthwhile objective.

Depending on your company, you may have significant leeway in formatting your deliverables, or you may need to stick to a very strict template. If you do have some flexibility, develop a set of personal templates that look professional. A small upfront investment will pay dividends in the long run since you won't have to reinvent them every time. Use the best sources at your disposal as references and borrow liberally until you have a solid base of your own from which to work.

In addition to visual presentation, consider how the content you deliver reflects on your personal brand. Just as a high-end retailer would not knowingly release poor-quality items into the market for fear of diluting its brand image, be careful not to publish anything that would detract from your personal brand. Even if it means working slower, and producing less in terms of pure volume, keep your focus on generating work that reflects the very best of your ability.

This approach may take longer initially, as you're ramping up your capacity to produce very high quality deliverables. However, once you develop a set of templates and hone the skill of distilling information down to its essence, you'll find that you can produce very high quality material in less time than it would have taken to assemble a more voluminous narrative of mediocre quality. Always be known for quality.

Keep Your Pants On

If love is the answer, could you please rephrase the question?

– Lily Tomlin

The second of Steven Covey's *7 Habits of Highly Effective People* is to "begin with the end in mind." Nowhere is this more applicable than the area of office romances.

Nothing has the potential to tarnish your reputation faster and more dramatically than getting involved with someone at work. Your office almost certainly has some kind of fraternization policy in place, and violating it carries with it the same risks as violating any policy. However, the consequences can stretch far beyond those of ignoring a typical company policy.

First, know that there are throngs of people engaged in daily drudgery who are dying for some hint of gossip. They view it as a fundamental human right to know what's going on in others' personal lives, especially if it can in any way be construed as salacious. They are so enamored by this possibility that even a hint of it can unleash a flurry of activity.

The trigger can be anything from a conversation overheard in the hallway to a chance weekend sighting. Even the suggestion of something happening can spark this pent-up demand for drama and make you the unwitting center of attention.

Typically it's a chain of events that leads to speculation, so there is no need to walk around the office dressed as a Puritan. But try to avoid anything that looks like an office romance, even if it isn't one. Dress modestly, speak respectfully and don't give people an excuse to read between the lines.

If there's nothing going on but you're maintaining an appearance that suggests otherwise, you're inviting attention and speculation. You should want people to recognize you for the great work you do, not because of rumors of extracurricular activities.

If there really is something going on, then consider that most relationships end unsuccessfully. When that happens, unlike relationships outside the office, it can be next to impossible to find distance. The situation can turn ugly fast and at best become a significant distraction.

While generally this principle falls under the category of "sound advice," there are a couple of scenarios that go even one step beyond. You must avoid without exception any fraternization with people to whom you report, and with any people who report to you. Even if the reporting relationships are not direct, meaning that there is someone separating the two of you within the management hierarchy, it's still an absolute no. Ignoring this could put you in serious legal jeopardy.

The same goes for relationships with suppliers, customers, government officials or other third parties where there is any kind of money changing hands or where influence could be beneficial. Not only could you put your job at risk, but you may also be violating the law.

It's OK to have fun at work. Don't be reluctant to develop strong, professional relationships with your colleagues. Just be smart and focus your romantic activities outside the workplace.

Always Be Learning

Judge a man by his questions, not by his answers.
— Voltaire

Always Be Closing is a sales philosophy championed by Alex Baldwin's character in the 1992 movie Glengarry Glen Ross. His character espouses a maniacal focus on closing sales, and refuses to accept excuses from anyone who fails to deliver.

It is in this spirit that the idea of *Always Be Learning* takes shape. If you can channel that same focus, energy and determination toward learning your craft, you will quickly become the smartest person in the room. Corporate America is full of people who believe that the only way they'll learn is by being trained. "I haven't been trained on that," they'll say. Or, "If they would just send me to a class maybe I would be up to speed on this stuff." That attitude will get you precisely nowhere. Monkeys are trained. Leaders learn in the moment, never passing an opportunity to pick up a new skill or tidbit of knowledge.

Never be afraid to show that you have things to learn, and are eager to learn them. Trying to hide your ignorance will only breed distrust and keep you from learning what you need to know. On the other hand, being open and even enthusiastic about what you don't know will endear you to others and send mountains of useful information your way.

The first step is to listen. Listen actively. Ask questions about what you don't know. In every meeting and conversation, write down anything you don't understand. Search the Internet or ask your colleagues for an explanation. Keep working until you understand everything you hear. It's OK if it takes a long time. Just be diligent about it and look at every meeting where you don't know something as an opportunity to learn.

Ask people for books, articles or blogs they think you should read. Ask them for a list of skills or areas that they think would be helpful for you to study, and get their advice on the best way to come up to speed on new or complex topics.

Pay attention to how people work, and try to adopt their best behaviors. Understand what makes people successful, and what does not. Practice emulating the best things you observe about people, even if it's something as simple as how they greet others.

Don't overlook what you can learn from people at all levels of the organization. You don't need to be in charge to have valuable skills. In fact, the people closest to you will often have skills and information that are most relevant to your job. Not everyone can be the CEO, but that doesn't mean they can't be great role models.

Keep a record of what you learn. Perhaps your company lacks a comprehensive list of its suppliers. By creating one you'll not only be learning about them yourself, but you'll be creating a valuable resource for others. As you continue to learn new things, take time to readjust your goals so that you always have something you're actively learning.

Make Your
Boss Successful

Don't worry when you are not recognized, but strive to be worthy of recognition.

– Abraham Lincoln

Your job is to make your boss successful. If something you're about to do fails to pass this test, then don't do it. It's better to do nothing.

This may seem old-fashioned. It doesn't mean you have to praise everything he does, or never push back when you disagree. In fact, in the right setting, being an honest sounding board can be hugely beneficial to your manager. It just means that your objective in all cases should be to make him successful.

Even if you don't trust your manager to return the favor and help make you successful, others will see this characteristic in you and want you to work for them. Managers don't just hire people to perform a task. In a larger sense they hire people to make them successful.

Don't try to outshine your boss. It's quite possible that you will, but trying will hurt your chances. Just focus on your job, and let more responsibility come to you.

Also consider that in a modern, matrixed organization you might have more than one boss, officially or otherwise. Endeavor to make all of your coworkers as successful as possible, regardless of whether or not you report to them.

When you become a manager, one of your roles will be to help the people that work for you be successful. In a way, you will be working for them, by helping them succeed. Consequently, this is a leadership trait that others will look for in you, before giving you the chance to lead. If you're focused only on yourself, then you're less likely to get that chance.

Become an Expert

It takes considerable knowledge just to realize the extent of your own ignorance.

– Thomas Sowell

The world relies on people who know things. Being able to assemble task lists, ask great questions and send out status updates are all valuable qualities, but there is a significantly greater benefit in becoming an expert at something yourself.

The number of subjects begging for experts is immense. It could be anything from a new piece of software, a new set of industry standards, or consumer trends within an emerging market. Pick something that's relatively new, of interest to you, and applicable to the work you're doing. Then, dive in and learn as much as possible.

Once I was part of a committee to organize an annual company conference. There was an emerging standard at the time called eXtensible Markup Language (XML), which everyone was interested in learning about. We discussed bringing in an outside speaker but didn't have the budget, so my friend and I volunteered to teach a class on the subject. We knew very little about it at the time. The fact that we had a defined audience and rapidly approaching conference date significantly increased the pressure for us to learn, and consequently we dove in and really did become experts in a short period of time. Not only did we present at that conference, but because of the popularity of the subject we taught a number of other groups as well. We started a knowledge sharing community on the topic and became known as experts within the company.

You can offer to conduct training on your chosen subject at work, write a guide, or volunteer to help whenever someone needs assistance in this area. Becoming an expert is a great way to get introduced to new people and interesting projects in a context that puts you in a favorable light.

Work When You're at Work

Concentrate all your thoughts upon the work at hand. The sun's rays do not burn until brought to a focus.

– Alexander Graham Bell

The new work style is to work whenever, wherever. The line between being at work and not being at work is becoming so thin as to be indistinguishable. Everyone you work with knows it. But they don't know that you know it. The only thing they know is what they observe, and they will be observing you at work. So work while you're at work.

People form opinions quickly, and they share those opinions with others. Don't give them an opportunity to think you're not working hard. Even if you become CEO, people will start to talk if they can't see that you're working hard, and that will impact the rest of the company.

Try not to let personal issues affect your work, especially when you're first starting out. Show up on time. Limit the amount of time you need to work from home. It's fine if you need to take some time now and again, but make sure your first priority is to establish a reputation for showing up and working hard.

If you do have something outside the office you need to take care of, don't try to hide it. The best approach is to address it head-on and be completely open about it. If people feel you're trying to hide something, then they'll suspect that you're making excuses. If you're open about it, they'll be more likely to empathize, since everyone has something come up from time to time that interferes with their normal work schedule.

Once I had a coworker who was notorious for being late to work. When asked he would mumble something about a sick cow, or a new pig being born. He seemed so cagey about it that no one really asked any details. "Does he live on a farm?" No one really knew for sure. We just thought he was weird. In retrospect, if he had come into the office at 10:00 with some pictures of a newborn colt or some other farm story, I'm sure everyone would have been amazed and considered him the hardest working member of the team. People would have been lining up at his desk to hear what had happened that morning, instead of talking behind his back. More often than not, people will treat you the way you treat you.

Emergencies aside, carve out the time you need to be at work and maintain a strong focus. Let someone else gain a reputation for being the office jokester, master socializer, or remote worker. It's too hard to reverse a negative first impression.

Turn Lead Into Gold

All things are difficult before they are easy.
– Thomas Fuller

Inevitably there will be some part of your job that you just don't like. And there may be times when the part of your job that you enjoy the least becomes your primary activity.

Assuming it's not something you can delegate, deprioritize, or defer, then you're going to have to find a way to power through it. Often the best approach is to figure out a way to go so far beyond expectations that it becomes a source of satisfaction.

For example, let's say you love performing experiments, but hate the drudgery of assembling reports. Make the best reports anyone has ever seen. Not just in your company, but anywhere. Reach out to colleagues and understand how they create reports. Start teaching other people how to make great reports. Learn how to write some basic software to automate report generation, or partner up with someone who can develop it for you. If you take it far enough, you'll be proud of what you're doing and it can eventually become a source of satisfaction.

Once I was assigned the dreaded task of assembling a set of policies and standards. No one reads internal policy documents. Most are boring, outmoded artifacts best suited for the shredder.

To combat my aversion to this task, I set out to assemble a standards document that I could be proud of – with the goal of having a copy on everyone's desk. I recruited some team members to work on it, which prompted energizing and engaging debate around how we should architect solutions within our company. Further, I decided to have the book published using an on-demand printing service so that it would look professional, and stand out from the reams of hastily printed material and oceans of digital documents in people's inboxes. Finally, since photography is one of my favorite hobbies, I spent some time to take a dramatic photo of our company headquarters and used that for the cover. The result is a book that still holds some notoriety years later, and is something I'm proud to keep on my bookshelf even though it's long since outlived its usefulness as reference material.

The key to applying this principle is to leverage your interests and strengths to turn an activity you hate into something you can be proud of.

Read What Others
are Reading

I cannot remember the books I've read any more than the meals I have eaten; even so, they have made me.

– Ralph Waldo Emerson

It sucks to be the last one to know something, especially when it's printed on the front page of a newspaper with a daily circulation of more than two million copies.

The preferred source of news is going to differ depending on where you work and what industry you're in, but there will usually be at least one. You should read it on a regular basis. At a minimum, scan the headlines before an important meeting. Even if you don't have time to dive into the details, you can at least avoid a look of total bewilderment when someone important asks what you think about your main competitor announcing an acquisition.

Often there is someone assigned to comb through news sources and produce a daily report for executives. If there is, you should ask to get access to that news summary. Typically this is a corporate communications function. Sometimes it's available to anyone via a company intranet, and sometimes it's distributed directly via email.

You can also create your own news summary by subscribing to alerts via Google News, Twitter or other online services. Think of keywords relevant to your company, competitors, customers, suppliers, and your industry generally.

Finally, it's always a good idea to ask people what they're reading or what they would recommend that you read. In addition to providing useful information, it's a good conversation starter when you're stuck talking with executives you don't know well. It shows ambition and curiosity without going over the top, and can give you valuable insight into how they think.

Ask for Feedback

Feedback is the breakfast of champions.
– Ken Blanchard

Most people are willing to give you helpful feedback on your performance if you ask. By asking for feedback in advance, you can turn any presentation or assignment into an opportunity for improvement. You can ask for feedback from anyone; it doesn't have to be your direct manager.

Most likely your company will have some formal process by which you'll receive feedback on your performance, usually on an annual basis. As a new employee you need to receive feedback more frequently than that. Managers are usually happy to spend the time, provided you have a sincere interest in listening and taking action.

Never let your formal end-of-year conversation be a surprise. It's OK to ask if you're on track for a good rating, and if there is anything you can do to improve your performance. Just make sure not to overdo it. Checking in on this once a quarter for an annual cycle is probably about right.

Asking for feedback from managers provides additional benefits. If they're thinking regularly about how you're performing and they know you're trying to do a great job, they'll feel more invested in your success. Often managers get the impression that their employees simply don't care about doing a better job. This especially applies to younger employees where there may be a bit of a gap in communication style. So, make sure your boss knows it's important to you to do a great job, and enlist her support in helping you get there.

Another effective way to get feedback is from customers, which could be internal or external to the company. You might simply ask them directly, solicit written comments, or even develop a survey. It's worthwhile to consider the merits of both qualitative and quantitative feedback, as well as both anonymous and attributable forms of input. This helps you create a good picture of what's going on, and establishes an effective benchmark for later improvements.

No matter what area of the business you're working in, understanding how your customers and other stakeholders feel about the work you're performing is critical to doing a great job.

Plan Ahead for Vacation

Only when the tide goes out do you discover who's been swimming naked.

– Warren Buffett

Depending on your job responsibilities, you may need to plan ahead for the time you'd like to take off.

First, in terms of how long to take and when, it's important to understand a company's culture. In some companies it's acceptable, and even encouraged, to take two weeks off at once, whereas at other companies so much happens in two weeks that to take more than one week at a time is considered excessive.

Some companies also have a particular month, such as August, when most people take their extended vacations. It's important to understand this and check with someone to see if that means you should try to take your vacation then also, or if you'll need to be in the office to cover for others. Also be aware of critical company meetings or events that you might need to schedule around. Ask if you're not sure.

Plan your time off as far in advance as possible. Of course things may come up unexpectedly, but whenever you can you should create a plan to make sure that everything runs smoothly while you're out of the office. Understand who will perform the functions you normally do, on a regular as well as emergency basis, and be sure that adequate cross-training and documentation are in place.

Set clear expectations about your availability when you're gone. You may decide that you're only available for emergencies, or you might decide that you'll try to stay as connected as possible. Usually it's best to disconnect as much as you can. Be aware that if you say you're unavailable, but then respond, you set the expectation that you'll continue to respond. If you must remain keyed into what's going on in the office, set a certain time each day to check in, and then resist the temptation to be available outside of that window.

When you come back, if there were problems that went unsolved, or if people failed to make as much progress as you anticipated, don't be upset. Take that as a sign that your presence in the office does in fact make a difference. Once we had a coworker leave for his honeymoon, having left some great instructions on what to do if something went wrong. By the time he came back things were running only at about 20% of normal capacity, and were in real jeopardy of failing completely. He thanked us for looking after his area while he was away and immediately started putting things back together. I have always been impressed by the maturity of his response.

The more you plan ahead and set expectations about your time off, the more you'll be able to relax and recharge. While that clearly has benefits for you, it's also important for the company that you gain some distance from your work. The best vacations are the ones where you don't think consciously about work at all, but upon returning find a new perspective on your day-to-day activities.

Consider the Total Cost

When you have a big, ugly problem, there's never going to be a neat, elegant solution that is totally painless or without a cost.

– Henry Paulson

Leaders hate to hear the words "it's free" when it's something their team is responsible for. In business, nothing is free.

Free conferences come with the cost of travel and time away from work. Free equipment comes with the cost to transport, install and eventually discard. Free software comes with the cost to host, manage, and upgrade. Freely obtained consumer information comes with the cost of storage, protection and legal compliance.

Time and time again I have seen inexperienced employees try to make the case that something can be produced, managed or maintained without a cost to the business. Every time they've been proven wrong.

Everything you do should have an overall net benefit to the company. This means spending money or investing some other resource, and gaining something in return that's worth more than what you invested. This is the right way to present an opportunity. If you minimize or ignore the costs, your proposal could get derailed as people spend all their time looking for the hidden downside, as opposed to focusing on the benefits. Being upfront about the total impact of a given initiative almost always helps to sell the idea.

Richard Stallman, one of the founders of the free software movement is famous for saying, "Free software is a matter of liberty, not price. To understand the concept, you should think of free as in free speech, not as in free beer." If anything in a business context is free, it is free as in speech.

Learn Every Name

The name of a man is a numbing blow from which he never recovers.

– Marshall McLuhan

People like to hear their own name. Using someone's name can build trust, strengthen relationships and boost confidence.

Most experts agree that the biggest problem in learning a name is hearing it in the first place. When meeting someone for the first time, most of us are so focused on blurting out our own name, that we completely forget to listen for the other person's name.

There are myriad books full of methods for learning and remembering peoples' names, and it's worth reading one. As a summary, most methods rely on a few basic steps. First, listen for the name and repeat it right away to make sure you have it correct. Ask for a spelling, whether your pronunciation is correct, or anything else that will give you a moment to process the name. If they offer a business card, see where they're from or where they work and try to make some comment to show that you're paying attention. When meeting more than one person at a time, don't be in too much of a hurry to move from one person to the next.

Second, try to make some connection between the name you've just heard and something that you already know or can readily observe. For example, if you meet Pauline and she's wearing a purple scarf, file away a reference to "Purple Pauline" before moving on to meeting someone else.

If you're in a meeting with people who haven't met before, it's common to go through introductions as a first item on the agenda. Write down each person's name, in order, on a piece of paper while introductions are made. This way even if you've forgotten the name of someone you just met face to face, you can simply look down at your notes and figure it out based on where they're sitting. Depending on how interesting the meeting is, you potentially have an hour or more to concentrate on learning everyone's name, as opposed to the three to five seconds you had at first introduction.

To help embed names in your long-term memory, keep a notebook or set of electronic contacts including details on how you met and any other relevant information. That way if you know you'll be meeting with someone, you can quickly look up what you learned last time. An outstanding natural ability for remembering names and personal details can be surpassed by consistent, diligent note taking.

Finally, use people's names whenever possible, whether you're asking a question in a meeting, asking for a favor, or just saying hello or goodbye. Focusing on just this one principle can yield enormous benefits and is worth the investment in time and energy.

Manage Your Own Career

Managing your time without setting priorities is like shooting randomly and calling whatever you hit the target.

– Peter Turla

One of the great corporate ironies is the inevitable human resources speech about managing your own career. They'll say, "It's up to you to chart your own path! You are the boss of you. Decide what you want and make it happen." That will be followed by a herd of people walking into their manager's office and saying what to the manager sounds like, "I want to milk goats in Costa Rica. That's where I see my career going."

The manager will then say, "Costa Rica is great. Sounds wonderful." And then proceed to either fire them so they can find a job milking goats in Costa Rica, or more likely completely ignore the conversation so that everyone can get back to work.

The truth is that it is up to you to manage your own career. That part is absolutely true. What they usually leave out is how to do it. First, you need to be realistic. Unless you work for an international cheese company, you're probably going to have to relegate your goat-milking to hobby status. So pick something that's realistic for your company, or find another company. But don't complain about the company just because your employer isn't a good match for you.

Once you have a realistic goal, it is your job to make it happen. It's not your job to ask someone else to make it happen – but to literally make it happen. How do you do that? It's very simple, but not always easy. You need to convince the right people that having you in your desired role would be best for *them*. That means focusing on their needs, not yours directly.

It might take a while. And it's definitely going to take some work. If you work in Receiving but decide you really want to work in Payroll, then the first step is to meet some people in this new area. Ask them about what kinds of jobs might open up, and what skills would be important for you to develop in order to qualify. Be nice and do your best to really get to know the people on the team. Good managers are always on the lookout for talented people, and they usually look to their own employees to tell them who would be a good hire and who would not.

Be careful not to be too aggressive. Being upfront about your aspirations is fine, but trying to push too hard will not help your cause. Just start to build connections, and most importantly, continue to deliver in your current assignment. This is the currency you'll be trading to get this new position. Even if you're not happy in your current role, and think you could perform much better in a new area, you need to continue to execute as best you can. If you do this, word will get around that you're doing a great job, and that you're interested in a role in another area, and as soon as an opportunity opens up, you'll be right where you need to be to take advantage of it.

Fix the Problem First, Then Find a Solution

Give me six hours to chop down a tree and I will spend the first four sharpening the axe.

– Abraham Lincoln

There is nothing quite like having an employee who listens to what you say, and then gets it done with speed and efficiency. However, absolute precision in following instructions can sometimes be less than ideal.

Let's say you're asked to interview everyone in your department, understand what kind of business metrics they look at on a regular basis, and then create a set of reports that contains those metrics. You immediately start to set up meetings, record and assemble critical information, create drafts, and so on. You did what your manager asked you to do, so what's wrong with that?

Here are some questions you might try to answer before jumping into such a task. Does anything already exist at your company relating to your project? In most instances, the answer is yes. Perhaps a few months ago someone did some work on it and has something to start from. Often you can find something in a partially finished state, full of useful information, even though it was never completed. Other times you'll find something that was completed a long time ago and simply needs to be updated. Never assume that because you were not given copies of this previous work, that it does not exist.

Second, is anyone else working on this right now? You might be surprised how often multiple people end up working on the same thing in isolation within a large company. Ask yourself who else might have an interest in your project and see if they're already working on it. If not, perhaps they would be willing to contribute to it.

Third, has the problem already been solved, either within the company or outside? Few business needs are truly unique. You might simply be able to search the Internet and find a great starting point. You might also reach out to vendors or friends and ask if they have anything to start from.

These are just a few examples of ways to be sure the problem statement truly addresses the need. Sometimes in an effort to be helpful, managers can be very specific about the way in which they ask for something, but in reality they just want it to be done as quickly as possible.

Discuss the approach with your manager to make sure you have the right balance between being smart about how you solve the problem and actually getting down to business and doing the legwork. If you overuse these techniques, people may get the impression that you think you're above getting your hands dirty and doing the work.

A good rule of thumb is to spend ten percent of the time allocated to a project looking for alternate means of getting it done. For a ten hour project, that means it's worth investing an hour to see if there is a better way before diving straight into it. On the other hand, for a project expected to take six months to complete it may be worth taking a week or two upfront to talk with others who have completed similar projects to make sure you're going about it in the best possible way.

If you strike the right balance you'll be some combination of strategist and go-getter. That's exactly where you want to be.

Maintain Personal Relationships

The problem with the rat race is that even if you win, you're still a rat.

– Lilly Tomlin

Depending on your company culture, it may be difficult to find enough time to develop and maintain relationships outside the office. In addition the sheer volume of work assigned, many companies are now offering additional incentives to stay connected longer, such as social events, side projects or free food.

Part of this is driven by research showing that employees are more effective when they can leverage informal relationships to get things done. A free dinner at 7:00 p.m. is also a strong motivator to stay a bit later, thus doing more work, and also networking with colleagues.

It's true that all of this can contribute to a more rewarding, and ultimately more productive work environment. However, make sure to develop and maintain connections outside the company as well. This has several advantages.

First, it gives you a place to go to get away from work. You'll be happier and more productive if you can get a fresh perspective from time to time. Sometimes the biggest breakthroughs come from stepping away from a problem.

Second, it gives you leverage. If all of your professional connections are tied to your current job, the opportunities to find your next job will be limited. Strive to maintain a network that's broad enough to offer new opportunities.

Lastly, and perhaps most importantly, it allows you to focus on permanent connections. It can be surprising how quickly most relationships fade as soon as you're no longer working together.

Eventually you will leave the company you're with, so focus on building relationships with family, close friends and neighbors. You'll be building a stronger network. Hopefully some of your coworkers will also become great friends, but if you maintain a diverse set of relationships then you'll be in good shape no matter what happens.

Embrace Skip-level Opportunities

Experience is not what happens to you; it's what you do with what happens to you.

– Aldous Huxley

In most large companies, executives will schedule so-called skip-level meetings to give them a chance to interact directly with people two levels or more below them in the organization. These sessions can be valuable for executives, since they can get feedback directly from people doing various types of work, versus those managing the work.

These opportunities can be valuable for you also, since it gives you a chance to showcase what you're working on. However, they can also be a disaster if you're not prepared.

Here are a few things you should know about these meetings. First, you were not chosen at random. They might tell you that you were, but you were not. Most likely your manager identified you as being high-potential, and that's why you were selected. Congratulations.

Second, while they may say that they want you to ask tough questions, you should only do so if you're prepared for a tough response. For example, let's say you overheard someone talking about how the stock price is low because the company is not being aggressive enough in entering China. It's fine to ask about that as a general question, but if you ask it in a challenging way, expect to get a response that challenges your knowledge of the both the company and the Chinese market. Nine times out of ten they'll know more about both than you do.

That doesn't mean that you have to only throw them softballs, such as the chronically overused "What do you think our biggest challenge is as a company?" line. You can ask real questions – just ask them in a way that is respectful and genuine.

Whatever topics you choose, you should always make sure to have at least one question prepared.

Third, don't mistake an opportunity to ask questions with an invitation to complain about how things are going. In almost every case it's better to use other channels to communicate that message. And by all means, don't say anything that you think would be a surprise to your manager.

All of the principles in this book are especially applicable during an opportunity like this. Make sure you have an elevator speech, since you'll likely be asked what you're working on. You should dress appropriately, know what's happening in the news that day, and maintain a positive tone.

These moments are like mini-accelerators that can increase, or decrease, your standing within the company at a more rapid pace than normal. If that makes you feel nervous or unprepared, take some time to think through what you'll say. It's fine to ask your manager for help, and it's worth taking as much time as you need to prepare. Remember that you were asked to participate for a reason – so someone must be happy with the work you're doing. As long as you're prepared to talk about it then you can look forward to a great experience and a valuable opportunity to meet with a senior leader at your company.

Build Things
That Last

It is not the strongest of the species that survive, nor the most intelligent, but the ones most responsive to change.

– Attributed to Charles Darwin

If you talk with people who've been working for a long time, they'll tell you everything is cyclical. What's old becomes new, and then becomes old again. Company initiatives have a way of being repackaged and resold, and new batches of recruits seem to work endlessly to solve what are essentially the same problems.

One reason for this is that industry trends are, in fact, often cyclical. But there is another, less productive reason: most problems aren't solved well. Whether because of restraints on time, budget, expertise or attention span, most processes and systems amount to a patchwork, developed only to the point of minimum viability. From there they start their swift and steady march toward obsolescence.

Your goal should be to build things that last. If you step away, whether it's from a project, or a product or process, will it survive? Too often people believe that if something requires their constant attention, then it is a positive indictor of their worth and that it helps to maintain their job security. While this may be true, it also sets a cap on upward mobility. If you're constantly looking after what you're currently responsible for, how will you find the time to be responsible for anything else?

The way to make things last is to make sure that they're well built starting from a solid foundation, with a large number of people involved. Even if you can build something yourself faster than with a group, creating a team helps to build roots across the organization. Having this army of people will increase the chances of your initiative's long-term viability, because there will be more people around to look after it, adapt it and defend it over time.

Making sure that things are stable, well organized, and thoroughly documented will demonstrate that you've built something that will last. The more you build things that last, the more likely you'll have your pick of what you'd like to build next.

Do What's Best for You

Everyone is a genius. But if you judge a fish by its ability to climb a tree, it will spend its whole life believing it is stupid.

– Albert Einstein

Many people will tell you never to refuse a promotion or special assignment. They'll tell you that if you do, you'll be passed over for the next one and you'll miss your chance forever. You'll be branded as someone who's not a "team player" and hit a career dead end.

It's true that if you've worked hard and have the chance to do something that's big, sounds exciting, and is likely to be successful, then there is no reason you should turn it down. However, if it's not important to the company, not something of interest, or mired in corporate politics then you're better off saying no.

You need to decide what's most important to you, and judge each opportunity on those merits. You might decide that making more money is your number one objective, and that you're willing to put up with any kind of assignment that satisfies that requirement. Most people regret that choice, but if that's what your heart tells you, then go for it.

For many, the best objective is to optimize the ratio between what you consider to be work and what you're paid. Everyone has a different definition of what constitutes work. For you, traveling two weeks a month might be lots of fun and hardly seem like work, whereas for others it might be torturous. So you'll need to calculate this for yourself, and when considering a new opportunity, perform an honest assessment of whether or not it will result in a better work to pay ratio.

It's also up to you to set the time period over which you make your determination. It's true that sometimes taking a somewhat painful assignment will qualify you for something that, in the long run, will result in a better job for you. Just make sure that the time horizon is not too long, and that the path is clearly visible. Temporary assignments have a way of becoming permanent, especially if you do a good job.

It's always difficult to say no, but by saying yes to what makes you happy you're likely to work harder and do a better job. If you're doing a great job, they'll still keep you in mind for the next big assignment. Sometimes you may not have a choice. But if they're asking, it means you do, and you should exercise that choice.

Find a "Make Me Famous" Project

Do not go where the path may lead, go instead where there is no path and leave a trail.

– Ralph Waldo Emerson

One of the sad realities of corporate life is that you can do a great job working on important things for a long time, and never really stand out. For some this might be fine, or even preferable. There's nothing wrong with being known as a solid performer who's willing to take on the work that no one else wants.

That said, if you want to advance your career as fast as possible – and have a shot at being at the top of the heap – you need a "make me famous" project. You'll know this project when you see it. It's the one that your boss, and her boss, and everyone else who matters cares about the most. It's often the most difficult, least defined and riskiest project.

So, why then would you to take it? First, it's the one everyone is paying attention to, so if you do a great job then everyone will notice. Second, most people will realize that it's really hard. That will both allow you some slack for when things don't go perfectly and also raise the stakes for when you deliver. Third, and most importantly, because it's the project your leadership team cares about the most, it's the one that they're most likely to step in and guarantee to be successful. If a smaller, easier project starts to falter they will pull resources away from that project and put it toward the one that's most important. You don't want to be in charge of the smaller, easier project when that happens.

The biggest challenge, naturally, will be getting yourself assigned to this project. The most obvious way to make this happen is to volunteer for it. Tell your boss that whenever there is something really big, even if it's really difficult, you're ready for it and willing to take it on. You might be surprised how much of a difference this makes.

Further, the more you can keep your current work under control, the more likely you are to get tapped for something new. Those that are always working right at the edge of their capacity often don't get chosen for the most important projects, because they're too busy with what they already have.

Barring an outright assignment to the project, the best approach is to find some backhanded way to get involved. Look for anything that can get you into a meeting, or responsibility for part of a deliverable, no matter how small. What starts as a small assignment can develop into something larger. Make sure to make this your top priority. Things tend to change very quickly on projects like this, and when they do they'll be looking for someone who has some familiarity with the project and who's done good work on it so far.

The project that brought me the most attention started with carving out some time from my day job, even though I didn't really have it. I managed to do just enough work to be invited to a kickoff meeting where I made a few suggestions that caught some people's attention. Based on that they asked me to develop my idea a bit further. As I started working with them on that idea, I became more exposed to the larger project, and they started to think more and more that I needed to be part of the team. That started on a part-time basis, and then when the person originally assigned to lead the project suddenly left the company, I was the natural choice to take her place.

Working on a project like this has its downsides, including long hours, frequent changes in direction and lots of people yelling at each other. However it also provides a number of benefits beyond just a year-end rating. It's on projects like this where you can really bond with coworkers. You're also more likely to interact with senior leaders within the company. You'll have some great stories to tell. And you might just become famous.

One note of caution. It's possible to become so connected to a project that you become permanently attached to it. You don't want to be known as a one-trick pony. I once worked with someone whose first name, at least within the office, literally became the name of the system he implemented – called Jupiter. Everyone called him Jupiter Jones, because he just never moved on to do anything else. To this day I can't even remember his real first name. Find the right project, deliver the hell out of it, and then go be famous doing something else.

Save for Retirement

Cannot people realize how large an income is thrift?

- Cicero

There is much that could be said, and has already been said about saving for retirement. Little can be gained by repeating it in great detail here. To keep it simple, I'll mention just four key principles to keep in mind.

The first is to start saving right away. Barring extraordinary circumstances, you should sign up for whatever kind of savings plan is available at work, usually a 401(k) if you're employed in the United States, via automatic payroll deduction. If your company provides a matching program, make sure you save enough to qualify for the full match. If you don't, you're declining money from your employer that you've already earned.

If you can, save the maximum allowed under pre-tax limits. By saving pre-tax you'll allow your savings to generate returns faster than if you save using post-tax dollars. Another popular option for American workers is a Roth IRA. If you qualify, it's a great way to save additional money on a pre-tax basis. The critical factor in all of this is to start immediately so that compound interest starts to work in your favor.

The second key principle is to diversify. Often your financial provider will offer tools to see if you're properly diversified, and if you have an appropriate risk profile. If not, you can also find tools online that will analyze your portfolio and make recommendations. It's a good idea to review your portfolio at least once a year and rebalance your holdings if necessary. Your savings plan may also have mutual funds that automatically diversify and rebalance your portfolio based on a target retirement age. These can be good options as long as the fees are reasonable.

Speaking of fees, this is the third area to watch. Over the lifetime of your investments, the fees that funds charge can make a huge dent in your earnings. Picking funds that have low fees will maximize your return. Index funds are a good option to keep fees in check.

Finally, don't withdraw your pre-tax funds unless you truly have an emergency, and don't stop your regular contributions. Just stay the course and let the market start to work for you.

If this sounds too complicated, it's worth finding someone to help. There may be free resources available to you at work. If not, it's worthwhile to spend money to talk with a financial advisor. Usually a one-time, fixed-fee consultation is enough to get you on a solid track. It's generally best to avoid paying management fees, especially if your investment needs are relatively straightforward.

Above all, don't let this potentially intimidating topic keep you from jumping in and getting started. If eighty percent of success in life is showing up, then eighty percent of success in investing comes from putting money aside and leaving it alone.

Be a Leader

Do not pray for easy lives. Pray to be stronger men.

– John F. Kennedy

Being a leader transcends title, age, experience and any other tangible characteristic. Being a leader is an action, and you can choose to be a leader just as much as anyone else, regardless of the circumstance.

Even in a situation where it's most appropriate to be a follower, you can still demonstrate leadership by being the first to follow. I remember a staff meeting where our manager announced a new policy from the corporate office saying that cell phones would no longer be provided by the company. Several coworkers instinctively clung to their phones, and a series of protests erupted. I immediately took my phone out of my pocket and slid it across the table. I let my boss know that coverage on my personal cell phone wasn't very reliable – which was true – but that she should feel free to try calling in the event of an emergency. "Why don't you hold on to your phone just for a while longer," was her response. The policy never took effect.

There is a difference between managing and leading. Managers compel people to complete tasks. It's often said that you lead from the front, whereas you manage from behind.

Leaders pick up the torch and start running. Your torch might be a whiteboard marker when someone needs to write down the ideas of the group. Your torch might be a late shift, or the early adoption of an initiative that seems in doubt. Your torch might simply be your opinion, voiced in a forum that may not initially be receptive to it.

A leader serves the group, and as such can never be overbearing, because he will never ask someone to do something he is not willing to do himself. Leaders demonstrate the principles they seek to develop in others. Leaders focus on the work at hand, instead of seeking for recognition. Leaders focus on what is right instead of what is popular.

I worked for a great leader once who worked so hard, and was so committed to the work he was doing, that he could ask anything of anyone. It was impossible to say no to him, because you knew that if you said no, he would find a way to get it done anyway, even if it meant doing it himself. He was full of energy and contagious enthusiasm. We all wanted to get things done for him. Even when people didn't agree with his specific direction, they wanted to be a part of it, because they could see that their work was part of something big and important, and in a way inevitable. He inspired great confidence in his team.

Leaders don't always work on the most visible or most critical part of a project. When everyone is working toward a big deadline, in my experience it's the most senior leader who takes on the responsibility of getting dinner or snacks for the team. I've probably witnessed some of the highest-paid pizza delivery people in history. It was important for them to show the team that they appreciated what they were doing, and that no task was beneath them. Whatever your function, and whatever your sphere of influence, be a leader.

Deliver

*Opportunity is missed by most people because it is
dressed in overalls and looks like work.*

– Thomas Edison

Above all else, deliver. Your objective should always
be to exceed expectations. Align with stakeholders on
what they expect, do your homework to make sure
it's achievable, and then do everything you can to
beat it. If you don't believe it's achievable, it's
imperative that you address that upfront. Once you
start working on something, you've made a
commitment. Break the work into pieces if necessary,
but always make sure that if you're working on

something, there is a clear expectation around when and how it will be completed.

If you've committed to finishing something by Friday, seek to finish it by Wednesday or Thursday. That gives you a bit of cushion in case something isn't quite right. If someone is expecting you to benchmark three companies, benchmark ten. If you're expected to build something for $100, look for a way to build it for $80.

The number one reason that top performers fail to meet or exceed expectations is that they set expectations too high. They're used to challenging themselves, and so they like to set the bar high. It feels great. But if everyone else promises ten bags of nuts, and you promise fifteen but deliver only twelve, then you've failed, because everyone was counting on fifteen. So even though you delivered 20 percent more nuts than anyone else, you're the one who hasn't met expectations. You might call it unfair, but it's a reality. Promise eight bags, have your boss give you a stretch assignment to get to ten, and then deliver twelve, and you'll be a hero.

It's not sufficient to merely deliver on-time. You need to meet or exceed expectations for the quality of the finished product. Make sure you proof-read, verify or test anything you pass along. Ask others to validate for you, especially if it's something you've never done before.

When you accept a deliverable, you are making a solemn promise. It doesn't mean that you'll try. In the words of Jedi Master Yoda, "There is no try." You must deliver. If you are known for anything, be known for delivering.

Pro basketball player Karl Malone was known as "The Mailman" because he always delivered. That's what you're going for. Of course on a daily basis you may occasionally fall short. But if you structure your objectives properly, set realistic expectations, and ask for help when you need it, you can become known for always coming through for the team.

Look for small ways to deliver, on a daily basis. Show up early for meetings. Make the extra effort to check in and see how your coworkers are doing. Ask your boss if there is anything you can do for him, even if you already have a full list of things to get done.

Only when people have total confidence in your ability to deliver your own work will they start to contemplate making you accountable for the work of others. This is known as a promotion, and it's a good thing. But it starts with making promises and then doing whatever it takes to keep them.

Made in the USA
Las Vegas, NV
12 September 2023

77418312R10115